Star Strains

Star Strains

Matthew Petchinsky

Star Strains: Exploring Astrology Through the Lens of Hemp
By: Matthew Petchinsky

Introduction – The Cosmic Plant Connection

For thousands of years, human beings have looked to the skies for guidance—and to the earth for healing. At the intersection of these two realms lies a truth both ancient and revolutionary: **plants are cosmic allies**, rooted in soil yet responsive to the stars. Among these botanical companions, *hemp* stands as a sacred conduit—one that bridges body and spirit, grounding and expansion, silence and awareness.

This book is born from that intersection: the vibrant meeting point where **astrology and hemp** not only coexist, but co-create healing, insight, and transformation.

Hemp as a Celestial Messenger

Often categorized simply as a wellness supplement or fiber crop, hemp is much more than a practical plant. It carries **vibrational intelligence**, shaped not just by climate and care, but by **celestial timing**. Ancient agricultural traditions knew this well. Farmers in both the East and West observed **lunar planting calendars**, recognizing that germination, flowering, and harvest responded best when attuned to moon phases and planetary transits. Hemp, with its sensitivity to environmental rhythm, responds potently to these cycles.

But hemp's story doesn't end in the fields—it begins anew in the **ritual space**, the **therapeutic setting**, and the **inner life** of the modern seeker.

Astrology as a Living Language of Energy

Astrology is not merely a system of personality traits—it's a **map of energy flow**. Each zodiac sign represents a unique blend of elemental force, planetary rulership, and developmental archetype. When you understand your natal chart, you understand how you move through time, intention, and transformation. But energy doesn't move in a vacuum—it needs a **vessel**.

This is where hemp enters.

Whether through full-spectrum CBD oil, smokable flower, topical applications, or ritual elixirs, **hemp serves as a physical gateway to astrological harmony**. It brings the intangible into the body. It allows you to embody your planetary energies—rather than just think about them.

Hemp and Ritual: A Forgotten History

Across cultures, the ritual use of hemp has long been associated with **altered states of consciousness, prayer, healing, and divination**. In ancient China, Taoist shamans utilized hemp incense during spirit journeys. In India, *bhang*—a preparation made from hemp leaves—was associated with sacred rites and festivals, especially those honoring Shiva, the god of transformation. In Scythian burial chambers, hemp smoke was used to commune with the dead and the stars alike.

These rituals were not merely cultural—they were **astrological acts**, timed with solstices, eclipses, and equinoxes. They used hemp to unlock the energy of celestial alignments, allowing humans to meet the stars in an embodied, felt experience.

A Modern Reawakening

Today, as both **astrology and hemp experience a global renaissance**, a profound truth is returning to light: these tools were never meant to be separate. Your nervous system, emotional body, and energetic field respond to lunar transits, solar flares, Mercury retrogrades, and Saturn returns. Hemp can serve as a stabilizing anchor—an **astro-integrative plant** that enhances your ability to **navigate your chart**, process cosmic shifts, and stay grounded in purpose.

Whether you're a fire sign seeking emotional calm, an air sign needing focus, a water sign craving protection, or an earth sign desiring higher insight, hemp offers specific support.

Why This Book Exists

Star Strains is not a how-to manual for hemp use or a dry astrological report. It's a **journey into embodied astrology**, where each chapter invites you to meet the signs through the healing, clarifying, and activating lens of hemp. You'll learn what strains complement your Sun, Moon, and Rising signs, how to use hemp to ease difficult transits, and how to ritualize your relationship with the stars.

More than that, you'll learn that **hemp is not just something you use**—it is a teacher, a mirror, and a partner.

This is not about escape. It's about alignment.

This is the **cosmic plant connection**.

And your journey through the zodiac just got a lot more grounded. Let's begin.

Chapter 1 – Aries & Activation: Hemp for Drive and New Beginnings

Aries is the zodiac's spark plug—the blazing ignition of the astrological wheel. Ruled by Mars, Aries governs beginnings, leadership, action, and personal willpower. It's raw, primal energy, often likened to a wildfire—fast-moving, courageous, and at times, uncontrollable. When harnessed, Aries brings initiative, bravery, and trailblazing creativity. When unbalanced, it can spiral into restlessness, impatience, aggression, and burnout.

Hemp, as an adaptogenic and nervine botanical, offers a natural counterbalance to Aries' intensity—**not by dampening its fire, but by refining it**. This chapter explores how specific strains and methods of hemp consumption can support Aries individuals (and those navigating Mars-heavy transits) in channeling their natural drive into sustainable, empowered action.

Understanding Aries Energy

- **Element:** Fire
- **Modality:** Cardinal (initiates energy)
- **Planetary Ruler:** Mars (assertion, war, motivation)
- **Body Rulership:** Head, brain, face
- **Strengths:** Courage, leadership, instinct, momentum
- **Challenges:** Impulsiveness, irritability, lack of follow-through, mental overload

Aries energy is fast and furious. It thrives on challenge but often burns itself out by sprinting toward a dozen goals at once without stopping to breathe. Aries may leap before they look—and while that can be admirable in situations of crisis or innovation, it can also lead to rash decisions, tension headaches, over-exertion, or emotional explosions.

Enter: hemp.

Hemp as an Aries Ally
Hemp offers Aries two key gifts:

1. **Grounding the Fire:** Aries often resides in the upper chakras—thinking quickly, speaking abruptly, acting immediately. Hemp helps bring this energy *downward*, anchoring it in the body so that passion becomes presence.
2. **Fueling the Spark Sustainably:** Instead of letting Aries run on fumes, hemp helps maintain steady creative flow, supporting recovery, focus, and long-term energy management without sedation.

Ideal Hemp Profiles for Aries

When selecting hemp for Aries, it's important to avoid strains that are overly sedating or mentally fogging. Aries doesn't want to be slowed to a crawl—it wants to be sharpened and stabilized.

Best effects to target:

- Anxiety relief without lethargy
- Increased focus and clarity
- Mild euphoria to stimulate creativity
- Pain and inflammation reduction (especially in head/neck)
- Nervous system regulation during stress

Recommended Cannabinoids & Terpenes:

- **CBD + CBG Combo:** Helps ease inflammation and boosts mental alertness
- **Limonene:** Uplifting, mood-enhancing, and anti-anxiety
- **Pinene:** Improves memory and focus, ideal for distracted Aries minds
- **Beta-Caryophyllene:** Balances overstimulation and helps modulate fiery emotional spikes

Top Strain Archetypes for Aries Activation
(Note: These are strain archetypes rather than branded names, so they may appear under different names in dispensaries or hemp suppliers.)

◈ "Solar Spark" (CBD/CBG hybrid)

Perfect for morning rituals and fresh starts. Clears brain fog while enhancing goal-setting focus.

◈ "Mars Balm" (High-CBD topical)

For Aries headaches, jaw tension, and facial inflammation. Apply before or after intense mental work or physical exertion.

◈ "Red Dawn Elixir" (Sublingual oil blend)

Used for harnessing creative drive during New Moons or Mars transits. Helps Aries move from chaos into conscious initiation.

◈ "Flashpoint" (Smokable strain with limonene/pinene blend)

Ideal pre-workout or pre-project spark without overstimulation. Best used in moderation to avoid restlessness.

Astrological Timing for Aries Hemp Use

- **New Moon in Aries:** Pair with a journaling ritual using a motivational strain to set bold new goals.
- **Mars Retrograde:** Use grounding strains to reflect and redirect your drive inward instead of pushing outward.
- **Mars Return (happens every ~2 years):** A potent time to realign your ambition—balance action with hemp-supported focus and restoration.

Daily Practice: Aries Activation Ritual
Materials:

- Hemp strain or oil from the suggested list
- Red candle or Mars talisman
- Peppermint or cinnamon essential oil
- Journal

Steps:

1. Light the red candle to honor Mars energy.
2. Inhale or apply your chosen hemp strain mindfully—focusing on intention, not escape.
3. Rub a small amount of peppermint or cinnamon oil onto your temples to awaken your mind.
4. Write for 7 minutes straight: "What do I want to begin today?"
5. Read your answer aloud with confidence, ending with: "And I move forward with balanced fire."

Embodying Aries Energy Without Burning Out

Hemp isn't here to dim your inner flame—it's here to **refine it**. Through mindful use, Aries individuals can experience:

- More follow-through on their ideas
- Better sleep after periods of high activity
- Reduced risk of injury from impulsive movement
- Calmer interpersonal dynamics without sacrificing assertiveness
- Enhanced clarity during high-stakes decisions

In truth, Aries doesn't need to slow down—it needs to **align** its fire with intention. Hemp provides the biochemical and energetic support to do just that.

Let your spark lead the way—but let hemp keep the fire from consuming the forest.

Chapter 2 – Taurus & Grounding: The Earthly Power of Hemp

Taurus is the embodiment of calm, embodied strength. As the second sign of the zodiac, ruled by **Venus** and governed by the **Earth element**, Taurus represents stability, sensuality, values, and the material world. It is the archetype of the **builder, nurturer, and preserver**—with a steady hand, a loving touch, and a deep appreciation for comfort and beauty.

Where Aries ignites, **Taurus roots**. It seeks not adrenaline, but **peace**, not a sprint, but a long, delicious stretch. And yet, in a fast-paced, anxious world, the Taurean spirit can be thrown off by overwhelm, overcommitment, or the pressure to perform. This is where **hemp becomes the perfect grounding agent**, helping Taurus reconnect with body, breath, and the joy of the present moment.

The Essence of Taurus Energy

- **Element:** Earth
- **Modality:** Fixed (sustains and maintains)
- **Planetary Ruler:** Venus (pleasure, beauty, values, embodiment)
- **Body Rulership:** Neck, throat, thyroid, vocal cords, and lower jaw
- **Strengths:** Patience, sensual wisdom, loyalty, resourcefulness, comfort-seeking
- **Challenges:** Stagnation, material fixation, resistance to change, emotional inertia

Taurus prefers a steady pace. It builds routines, creates beauty, and anchors others—but when imbalanced, Taurus can become overly rigid, attached to the familiar, and resistant to growth. At its worst, it may avoid discomfort entirely, suppressing emotions beneath a veneer of calm or indulgence.

Hemp, especially in its more soothing and body-nurturing forms, is a powerful tool for Taurus to re-center, process slowly, and emerge stronger, more grounded, and reconnected to joy.

Why Hemp Works So Well for Taurus

Taurus thrives on **sensory experience**—texture, taste, aroma, sound, and touch. Hemp offers a multi-sensory path to healing and grounded empowerment.

Hemp Supports Taurus By:

- **Calming the nervous system** after overstimulation
- **Soothing the throat chakra**, encouraging expressive and honest communication
- **Reducing physical tension** in the neck, shoulders, and jaw—common Taurus stress points
- **Enhancing sensory pleasure** during rituals, baths, massage, or mindful eating
- **Helping Taurus navigate change** with grace rather than resistance

Ideal Hemp Profiles for Taurus Energy

Unlike fiery signs, Taurus benefits most from **deep, earthy, and full-bodied hemp experiences**—whether smoked, infused, or applied topically.

Key effects to target:

- Muscle relaxation
- Emotional comfort and safety
- Enhanced sensual awareness
- Thyroid and hormonal support (via endocannabinoid system)
- Root chakra alignment and security

Recommended Cannabinoids & Terpenes:

- **CBD + CBC Combo:** Gentle mood support, body ease, and hormonal regulation
- **Myrcene:** Sedative and muscle-relaxing—great for evening wind-down
- **Linalool:** Enhances pleasure and reduces inflammation, associated with Venus
- **Beta-Caryophyllene:** Earthy, grounding, and anti-inflammatory—perfect for stubborn tension

Top Strain Archetypes for Taurus Grounding
(These are archetype-style profiles, and actual strain names may vary.)

◈ **"Velvet Root" (High CBD + myrcene-rich)**
Perfect for full-body relaxation after a long day. Best enjoyed in a warm bath, with candles and soothing music.

◈ **"Green Temple" (Balanced CBD/CBG blend)**
Ideal for restorative yoga, vocal therapy, or slow, mindful mornings. Supports thyroid health and voice clarity.

◈ **"Golden Garden" (Edible-infused)**
Taurus loves taste. A mild hemp edible paired with intentional savoring enhances both digestion and grounding.

◈ **"Earthsong Balm" (Topical)**
For the neck and shoulders—especially when carrying emotional weight. Massage into tense areas while listening to harmonic or instrumental music.

Astrological Timing for Taurus Hemp Use

- **Full Moon in Taurus:** Deep release of emotional or financial tension. Pair with a body oil ritual or sleep-focused strain.
- **Venus Transits:** Tune into sensual rituals with gentle strains and beauty-enhancing self-care (face masks, oils, aromatherapy).
- **Taurus Season (April–May):** Create consistent hemp rituals for grounding, prosperity mindset, and nervous system balance.

Taurus Ritual: The Sacred Senses Ceremony
Materials:

- Favorite strain or hemp oil
- A soft blanket or robe
- Fresh fruit, chocolate, or a favorite earthy tea
- Crystal: Green aventurine or rose quartz
- Music: Acoustic or nature-based

Steps:

1. Create a cozy, quiet space. Dim the lights. Wrap yourself in softness.
2. Inhale or sip your hemp product slowly. Let it settle into your body.
3. One by one, stimulate your senses—sip the tea, taste the fruit, touch the fabric, feel the music, gaze at a candle flame.
4. Reflect: "What does comfort mean to me?"
5. Write one thing you can do this week to cultivate sustainable pleasure without guilt.

This ritual reminds Taurus that comfort is not laziness—it is preparation for sustainable strength.

Embodying Taurus Wisdom Through Hemp

Taurus teaches that **power doesn't have to roar**—sometimes it's in the quiet, persistent presence of your breath, your skin, and your values. With the aid of hemp, Taurus energy can:

- Feel emotionally safe without emotional suppression
- Enjoy life's pleasures without overindulgence
- Express truths with clarity and warmth
- Heal physical stress stored in the throat and spine
- Attract prosperity through grounded embodiment

Taurus reminds us: **Slow is sacred.** And hemp helps us remember how to move at the speed of nature.

Chapter 3 – Gemini & Communication: Mindful Expression with Hemp

Gemini, ruled by Mercury and associated with the **Air element**, is the thinker, communicator, and connector of the zodiac. It governs ideas, language, curiosity, and the nervous system. Gemini's mind is fast—darting between thoughts like a hummingbird between flowers. This makes Geminis excellent at multitasking, absorbing information, and thinking on their feet. But that same speed can create scattered attention, anxiety, and burnout.

This chapter explores how **hemp becomes a vital tool for Gemini**—not to silence their minds, but to *focus* them. Rather than dulling mental activity, hemp can guide Gemini toward clarity, mindfulness, and effective communication by stabilizing the nervous system and enhancing presence.

The Essence of Gemini Energy

- **Element:** Air
- **Modality:** Mutable (adaptable, shifting)
- **Planetary Ruler:** Mercury (communication, thought, intelligence)
- **Body Rulership:** Lungs, hands, arms, shoulders, and the nervous system
- **Strengths:** Wit, flexibility, intellectual curiosity, expressiveness, sociability
- **Challenges:** Mental overstimulation, overthinking, superficial focus, anxiety, inconsistency

Gemini thrives on variety and speed. But too much input can lead to nervous system overload, shallow breathing, racing thoughts, and emotional disconnection. Hemp, when used intentionally, becomes a **mental tuning fork**—sharpening cognition while calming the reactive mental chatter that can leave Geminis exhausted.

Why Hemp Is Ideal for Gemini Minds

For Gemini, **balance is everything**. They need stimulation, but not chaos. Calm, but not sedation. Clarity, not fog. Hemp, especially in light daytime-use strains or nootropic cannabinoid blends, gives Gemini the best of both worlds.

Hemp Supports Gemini By:

- **Reducing nervous energy** and scattered thinking
- **Supporting lung health** through anti-inflammatory properties (important for an air sign)
- **Enhancing verbal clarity** for communication and writing
- **Encouraging mental stillness** without suppressing intelligence
- **Promoting mindfulness** in high-speed conversations or information-heavy tasks

Ideal Hemp Profiles for Gemini Energy

Gemini should avoid heavy indica-style strains or overly sedative cannabinoids unless it's for sleep. During the day, they benefit most from **mentally energizing, focus-enhancing, and socially supportive strains.**

Best effects to target:

- Mental clarity
- Verbal fluency
- Calm focus
- Anxiety reduction without drowsiness
- Balanced breathing and voice control

Recommended Cannabinoids & Terpenes:

- **CBD + CBG Combo:** Mental clarity with emotional grounding
- **Limonene:** Elevates mood and aids social engagement
- **Pinene:** Supports memory retention and cognitive clarity
- **Terpinolene:** Mildly energizing, helps with task switching and idea integration

Top Strain Archetypes for Gemini Focus & Flow
(Note: These are archetype profiles. Specific strain names may vary by source.)

◈ **"Airline Clarity" (CBD/CBG with pinene and limonene)**
A daytime strain for writers, speakers, and thinkers. Reduces stress while enhancing focus and articulate expression.

◈ **"Mercury Mind" (Sublingual tincture)**
Ideal for public speaking, interviews, or social anxiety. A few drops before a conversation help Gemini access clear, confident flow.

◈ **"Twin Bloom" (Smokable herbal blend)**
Blends hemp flower with supportive herbs like lavender and gotu kola. Perfect for balancing the "twin minds" and integrating multiple perspectives.

◈ **"Gemini Glide" (Inhalable vapor pen)**
For Geminis on the go. Supports breathwork, multitasking, and ease during travel, networking, or transitions.

Astrological Timing for Gemini Hemp Use

- **New Moon in Gemini:** Set intentions for mindful communication. Use a writing-friendly strain and journal new ideas.
- **Mercury Retrograde:** Hemp can reduce anxiety and boost reflection. Use calming blends for rethinking and revising plans.
- **Gemini Season (May–June):** Time to upgrade your communication rituals. Use hemp to support learning, socializing, and breath alignment.

Gemini Ritual: The Breath-and-Words Practice
Materials:

- Light hemp strain (tincture or smoke)
- Journal and pen
- Peppermint tea (for vocal clarity)
- Breath-focused background music
- Blue crystal: blue lace agate or aquamarine

Steps:

1. Inhale or ingest your hemp product while listening to steady, calming music.
2. Sip peppermint tea and breathe deeply, placing one hand on your chest and one on your throat.
3. In your journal, complete this prompt:
   - *"What words do I need to speak, write, or release today?"*
4. Speak your answer aloud, slowly and with intention.
5. Practice 3 rounds of **4-4-6 breathwork** (inhale 4, hold 4, exhale 6) to center the nervous system.

This ritual reminds Gemini that *clear speech comes from deep breath*—and that true expression begins with mindful presence.

Gemini Wisdom: Speak to Connect, Not to Impress

Gemini is not here to overwhelm others with words—it's here to **build bridges of understanding**. When Gemini energy is aligned, it brings laughter, insight, and connection to any room. When unbalanced, it can become fragmented, forgetful, or anxious.

With hemp's support, Gemini can:

- Finish conversations and projects without mental burnout
- Speak from grounded clarity rather than reactive emotion
- Strengthen lung health through breath rituals
- Reduce social anxiety and find joy in expression
- Integrate both minds—the intellect and the intuition

Gemini reminds us that **words are spells**, and every sentence can carry healing. Hemp is the herbal assistant that helps those words land, gently and clearly.

Chapter 4 – Cancer & Comfort: Nurturing the Emotional Self

Cancer, the fourth sign of the zodiac, is where emotion becomes sacred. Ruled by the **Moon**, governed by the **Water element**, and associated with **intuition, memory, and the inner child**, Cancer is deeply connected to feeling, protection, and the sacred space of home. It is both a healer and a keeper of emotional legacies, carrying the psychic tides of generations in its soft but strong shell.

And like the Moon it's ruled by, **Cancer is cyclical**. Emotions swell and recede, moods shift with unseen rhythms, and memories echo through the body. For Cancer, feeling deeply is a gift—but one that can become overwhelming without grounding practices and soothing support.

Hemp offers that support. Not just as a plant that relaxes the body, but as an emotional stabilizer, a sleep enhancer, and an intuitive amplifier. This chapter explores how **hemp becomes a spiritual balm** for Cancer—helping them hold space for others without losing themselves, and navigate their own inner ocean with clarity and compassion.

The Essence of Cancer Energy

- **Element:** Water
- **Modality:** Cardinal (initiating emotion and care)
- **Planetary Ruler:** Moon (emotions, cycles, motherhood, intuition)
- **Body Rulership:** Stomach, breasts, chest cavity, womb, and parasympathetic nervous system
- **Strengths:** Nurturing, empathetic, emotionally intelligent, intuitive, protective
- **Challenges:** Mood swings, emotional repression, hypersensitivity, fear of abandonment

Cancer's energy is soft but not weak. It's the energy of sacred containers—of homes, wombs, kitchens, altars. But because Cancer absorbs so much from others, it can suffer from emotional exhaustion, anxiety, insomnia, and psychosomatic tension. It may retreat into isolation or develop unhealthy comfort patterns to feel safe again.

Hemp is an herbal comfort blanket, helping Cancer return to a state of nervous system safety while preserving access to deep inner knowing.

Why Hemp is a Cancerian Ally

Cancer's needs are both emotional and physical. It needs calm. It needs comfort. It needs sleep, soothing textures, warmth, and gentle rhythm. Hemp addresses these needs holistically by interacting with the **endocannabinoid system**, especially where emotion, digestion, and sleep are concerned.

Hemp Supports Cancer By:

- **Easing anxiety and emotional intensity** without blunting sensitivity
- **Promoting restful, regenerative sleep**
- **Soothing stomach upset and stress-induced digestion issues**
- **Enhancing intuitive and dream states**
- **Creating sacred routines that foster emotional regulation**

Ideal Hemp Profiles for Cancer Energy

Cancer benefits most from **calming, body-centered, and sleep-enhancing hemp strains**. These should calm the nervous system, deepen breath, and ease the heart without mental sedation that feels numbing.

Best effects to target:

- Deep relaxation without emotional suppression
- Sleep onset and sleep quality support
- Gentle enhancement of dream states and intuitive insights
- Hormonal and gut-related balance (linked to mood)
- Comfort during emotional processing or grief

Recommended Cannabinoids & Terpenes:

- **CBD + CBN Blend:** A gentle sedative for sleep, grief, and emotional reset
- **Linalool:** Calms stress and eases insomnia (also found in lavender)
- **Myrcene:** Great for body relaxation and restful nights
- **Humulene:** Grounding, anti-inflammatory, helps with emotional eating triggers

Top Strain Archetypes for Cancer Comfort & Sleep

(Note: These are conceptual strain profiles. Actual names vary.)

◈ **"Moonmilk" (CBD + CBN dominant with myrcene and linalool)**

Ideal for nighttime rituals and grief recovery. Brings a sense of security and emotional release.

◈ **"Sea of Stillness" (High-CBD tincture with humulene)**

Soothes the stomach and solar plexus—perfect for Cancer's gut-based emotional processing. Use before meals or meditation.

◈ **"Wombsong" (Infused bath soak with hemp oil and lavender)**

Cancer heals best in water. This bath blend helps cleanse emotional residue and relax the heart.

◈ **"Lunar Lullaby" (Vaporizer blend or gentle tea)**

Supports dreamwork and Moon phase rituals. Great during New or Full Moons to amplify intuitive downloads while staying grounded.

Astrological Timing for Cancer Hemp Use

- **New Moon in Cancer:** Use hemp to create a new emotional foundation. Combine with journaling or vision board work focused on home, self-care, and feelings.
- **Full Moon in Cancer:** An emotional high tide—release tears, honor memories, and cleanse the body with soothing hemp strains.
- **Cancer Season (June–July):** Build emotional self-care rituals with hemp-infused oils, sacred baths, and sleep routines to enhance receptivity and calm.

Cancer Ritual: The Comfort Cocoon Ceremony
Materials:

- Weighted blanket or soft robe
- Hemp-infused bath soak or tincture
- Chamomile or warm oat milk drink
- Blue candle (for emotional peace)
- Crystals: Moonstone or selenite

Steps:

1. Take a warm bath or sip a calming hemp tincture.
2. Light the candle and wrap yourself in a blanket or robe.
3. Hold your crystal and repeat: *"I am safe in my softness. I am allowed to feel."*
4. Write a short letter to your inner child or younger self.
5. Place the letter under your pillow and drift into a guided sleep meditation or soft music.

This ritual helps Cancer release the day's emotional residue and find sanctuary within.

Cancer Wisdom: Softness Is Strength

Cancer's power lies not in walls, but in **boundaries infused with love**. It reminds us that protecting our energy is a sacred act—and that tenderness is not weakness, but a form of divine resilience.

With the aid of hemp, Cancer can:

- Sleep deeply and awaken emotionally restored
- Navigate emotional tides without drowning
- Maintain empathy while strengthening energetic boundaries
- Heal the nervous system after caretaking or emotional labor
- Amplify dreams, intuition, and lunar wisdom without losing balance

Cancer teaches that home is not just where we live—it's what we build inside ourselves. Hemp becomes part of that internal sanctuary, a quiet medicine for a loud world.

Chapter 5 – Leo & Confidence: Radiance Through the Hemp Lens

Leo, the fifth sign of the zodiac, is the sovereign of self-expression. Ruled by the **Sun** and powered by the **Fire element**, Leo represents confidence, passion, generosity, and the radiant force of the heart. It is the sign of performers, artists, leaders, and those whose purpose is to illuminate the world by simply being fully themselves.

But even the brightest stars can cast shadows.

Leo's strength lies in **visibility and creative courage**, but its wounds stem from **insecurity, fear of rejection, and the need for validation**. When the heart is unbalanced or the ego overcompensates, Leo can become overly prideful or quietly self-doubting—fearing that if they shine too brightly, they'll be judged, or worse, ignored.

Hemp, when used intentionally, becomes a *balancer of the Leo flame*—helping soften ego defensiveness, open the heart, and encourage grounded creative power. It nurtures Leo's inner child and reminds them that **true confidence comes not from applause, but from alignment.**

The Essence of Leo Energy

- **Element:** Fire
- **Modality:** Fixed (sustaining, stabilizing)
- **Planetary Ruler:** The Sun (identity, life force, expression)
- **Body Rulership:** Heart, spine, upper back, and circulatory system
- **Strengths:** Charisma, creativity, generosity, leadership, warmth
- **Challenges:** Ego sensitivity, attention-seeking, pride, fear of irrelevance

Leo's journey is to evolve from performance to presence—from needing to be *seen* to being *true*. And that's where **hemp becomes an ally**: It quiets the noise of comparison and reconnects Leo with their authentic radiance.

Why Hemp Empowers Leo's Confidence

Leo is here to express, to create, and to love boldly. But those gifts require **emotional openness and a regulated nervous system**. When Leo feels attacked, abandoned, or unseen, it may lash out, retreat, or perform to please. Hemp gently dissolves the walls of fear, allowing Leo to access a stable sense of self-worth that isn't dependent on others.

Hemp Supports Leo By:

- **Reducing anxiety around public visibility and performance**
- **Regulating heart-centered emotional energy**
- **Enhancing creativity without mental overstimulation**
- **Encouraging rest and nervous system reset after being "on" too long**
- **Opening the heart chakra while softening ego-based defensiveness**

Ideal Hemp Profiles for Leo Radiance

Leo benefits from hemp strains that support **confidence, clarity, creativity, and heart-centered relaxation**. The goal is to **enhance vitality without dulling self-expression**.

Best effects to target:

- Energizing clarity without anxiety
- Mood elevation and warmth
- Social ease and performance confidence
- Heart and spine tension release
- Restorative recovery after overstimulation

Recommended Cannabinoids & Terpenes:

- **CBD + THCv (non-intoxicating):** Promotes energy and confidence
- **Limonene:** Uplifting, citrusy, and emotionally expansive
- **Beta-Caryophyllene:** Grounds over-excitability and eases performance nerves
- **Linalool:** Balances strong emotions, perfect for Leo's dramatic internal landscape

Top Strain Archetypes for Leo Brilliance & Balance
(Conceptual profiles; strain names vary by supplier)

◈ "Solar Bloom" (CBD + THCv daytime blend)

A motivational, euphoric strain for Leo's creative process. Excellent for content creators, public speaking, and stage performance.

◈ "Heartfire" (High-CBD flower with limonene)

Brings warmth to the heart chakra, promotes courage to speak truth, and helps release fear of rejection.

◈ "Golden Rest" (CBD + linalool tincture)

Restorative support for Leos recovering from burnout, emotional drama, or too much "external energy." Best used at night.

◈ "Crown & Root" (Topical balm for spine and chest)

Massage into upper back and heart area to realign Leo's posture, breath, and energetic presence before facing the public or reflecting in solitude.

Astrological Timing for Leo Hemp Use

- **New Moon in Leo:** Set intentions for creative projects and inner child healing. Use heart-opening strains for journaling, drawing, or dancing.
- **Full Moon in Leo:** Celebrate yourself. Use uplifting strains to host or attend gatherings that honor your growth and joy.
- **Leo Season (July–August):** Lean into your visibility and build daily hemp-supported rituals for courage, rest, and radiance.

Leo Ritual: The Sovereign Self Ceremony
Materials:

* Hemp tincture or smokable flower (Solar Bloom or Heartfire recommended)
* Gold or orange candle
* Rose or jasmine essential oil
* Mirror
* Creative tool: pen, paintbrush, musical instrument
* Crystal: Citrine or sunstone

Steps:

1. Light your candle and inhale your chosen hemp strain.
2. Gaze into the mirror. Speak aloud: *"I am radiant, even when unseen. My light is real."*
3. Apply a few drops of rose or jasmine oil to your heart and wrist.
4. Create something—free write, draw, sing, or move your body. Don't edit or judge.
5. Place the citrine on your solar plexus as you rest, affirming:
   "I give myself the permission to shine from my soul, not my wounds."

Leo Wisdom: Lead from the Heart, Not the Wound

Leo is not about ego in the traditional sense—it's about becoming **a radiant force of healing by embodying joy**. But to lead with heart, the heart must be nourished. Hemp helps remove the tension around performance and allows Leo to speak, create, and connect from a space of authenticity.

With consistent, mindful use, Leo can:

- Heal from past rejection and reawaken creative passion
- Experience joy without needing external applause
- Perform or lead with clarity and presence
- Release emotional chest tension and performance anxiety
- Restore nervous system strength after emotional peaks or over-stimulation

Leo reminds us that true leadership comes from love, not fear. And **hemp helps make that love sustainable**.

Chapter 6 – Virgo & Healing: Precision, Routine, and Clean Green Energy

Virgo, the sixth sign of the zodiac, is the healer, the organizer, and the sacred server. Ruled by **Mercury**, Virgo embodies **earth-based intelligence**—it's the sign that wants everything to *work better*, from your digestive system to your calendar to the planet itself. With a focus on **refinement, purification, and practical wellness**, Virgo channels its energy into meaningful structure and detailed attention.

Virgo doesn't just "use" hemp—it **integrates it**. Every capsule, tincture, or topical is selected with intention. The Virgoan relationship with hemp is precise, clean, and rooted in the question: *How can this plant make my mind, body, and life more efficient and well-balanced?*

This chapter explores how hemp supports Virgo's need for clarity, physical healing, digestive health, and focused routines—**without disrupting their workflow or overwhelming their senses.**

The Essence of Virgo Energy

- **Element:** Earth
- **Modality:** Mutable (adaptive and flexible)
- **Planetary Ruler:** Mercury (intellect, systems, communication)
- **Body Rulership:** Digestive tract, intestines, gut-brain axis, spleen
- **Strengths:** Analytical thinking, precision, discernment, service-oriented, humility
- **Challenges:** Overthinking, perfectionism, worry, hypersensitivity to toxins, burnout from overworking

Virgo is the sign of systems. When balanced, it's efficient, grounded, and holistic. But when stressed, Virgo energy can become critical, obsessive, and tense. Its natural desire for cleanliness can become rigid; its gift for analysis can spiral into anxiety.

Hemp provides Virgo with what it most needs: gentle regulation, clean nourishment, and body-centered calm that supports productivity rather than disrupts it.

Why Hemp Aligns with Virgo's Wellness Ethos

Virgo rules the **gut-brain connection**, making it one of the most sensitive signs in the zodiac when it comes to inflammation, stress-related digestion issues, and mental burnout. This makes hemp an ideal ally—particularly when approached through **daily, ritualized, low-to-moderate dosing**, with a focus on *consistency and biofeedback*.

Hemp Supports Virgo By:

- **Reducing digestive inflammation and regulating gut health**
- **Providing anxiety relief without sedation**
- **Enhancing focus and mental clarity**
- **Calming perfectionistic thought spirals**
- **Supporting daily self-care through habit and structure**

Virgo wants *function*, not escape. And hemp, when selected intentionally, provides exactly that.

Ideal Hemp Profiles for Virgo Energy

Virgo benefits most from **clean, anti-inflammatory, and productivity-friendly hemp strains**, often in **tincture, capsule, or topical form** to avoid smoking or overly "loose" delivery methods.

Best effects to target:

- Digestive support and gut soothing
- Mental focus with calm undercurrent
- Inflammation reduction, especially in the intestines or joints
- Ritual-friendly formats (timed dosages, blends with herbal allies)
- Light body relaxation that doesn't impair performance

Recommended Cannabinoids & Terpenes:

- **CBD + CBC Blend:** For mood stability and digestive relief
- **Pinene:** Supports alertness and respiratory clarity
- **Beta-Caryophyllene:** Strong anti-inflammatory, particularly for gut and immune support
- **Ocimene:** Uplifting, antiviral, great for clean energy and gentle motivation

Top Strain Archetypes for Virgo Function & Flow
(Conceptual strain archetypes; actual strain names may differ by supplier)

◈ **"Clean Slate" (High-CBD with beta-caryophyllene & pinene)**
Perfect for morning rituals, spreadsheets, and structured writing. Enhances clarity while reducing inflammatory stress responses.

◈ **"DigestEase" (CBD tincture with CBC + ginger extract)**
Designed for Virgo's sensitive gut and gut-brain axis. Great before meals, after stressful days, or post-exercise.

◈ **"Green Code" (CBD capsule blend with adaptogens)**
Ritualized daily use capsule for productivity and focus. Contains no intoxicating compounds—perfect for wellness-focused Virgos.

◈ **"Pure Earth Balm" (Topical hemp salve)**
Soothes inflammation, especially in stomach, back, and hands. Use during quiet breaks, breathwork, or after chores and service work.

Astrological Timing for Virgo Hemp Use

- **New Moon in Virgo:** Reset your body, schedule, and systems. Use clarity-enhancing hemp to support a "clean start" in your habits or health goals.
- **Full Moon in Virgo:** Time to release perfectionism. Use hemp to aid in emotional digestion, detox from overthinking, and rest your body.
- **Virgo Season (August–September):** Build sacred rituals of hemp use tied to your body's needs, productivity goals, and digestive peace.

Virgo Ritual: The Precision Wellness Practice
Materials:

- Journal or health tracker
- Hemp tincture or capsule
- Herbal tea (peppermint, dandelion, or lemon balm)
- Timer or planner
- Green or white candle

Steps:

1. Take your hemp tincture or capsule with warm tea.
2. Light your candle and sit in a quiet, clean space.
3. Set a timer for 10 minutes and reflect:
   "What needs purification in my body or schedule?"
4. Write 3 small changes you can make this week to support your health.
5. Organize those tasks in your planner, with checkboxes to track progress.
6. End with a breath practice: *inhale structure, exhale tension.*

This ritual honors Virgo's love for **clean systems and sacred wellness,** and invites hemp into that space as a supportive collaborator.

Virgo Wisdom: Ritual is the Root of Healing

Virgo teaches that health is built in moments—choices, patterns, and habits that align with your core values. It's not about perfection, but **precision in presence**. Hemp can be a quiet companion in that process—helping Virgo find mental clarity, digestive balance, and emotional regulation.

With consistent use, Virgo can:

- Build healthy rituals with measurable benefits
- Improve gut and immune system response
- Relax their perfectionistic mind without losing momentum
- Return to the body with compassion and structure
- Serve others from a place of energetic fullness

Virgo reminds us: **Healing is sacred structure**. And hemp, when used intentionally, becomes a plant-powered part of your daily architecture of wellbeing.

Chapter 7 – Libra & Balance: Hemp in Harmony and Relationships

Libra, the seventh sign of the zodiac, is the diplomat, the artist, and the sacred mirror. Ruled by **Venus** and aligned with the **Air element**, Libra is concerned with **balance, aesthetics, justice, and connection**. It is the sign of relationships—not only romantic, but also social, professional, and internal. Libra's purpose is to harmonize the world around it, often acting as a bridge between opposing forces.

But this grace comes with complexity.

Libra is often caught in the middle—**weighing, reflecting, adapting**, sometimes to the point of indecision or self-sacrifice. While Libra craves equilibrium and beauty, it can be plagued by anxiety, overthinking, or emotional imbalance in chaotic environments. And because it's an air sign, its nervous system is prone to overstimulation in the pursuit of "peace."

This is where **hemp steps in as a graceful stabilizer**. Libra doesn't want to feel dulled—it wants to feel aligned. Hemp, when used intentionally, helps Libra quiet the external noise, clarify their needs, and re-enter the world from a place of **inner poise and heartfelt presence**.

The Essence of Libra Energy

- **Element:** Air
- **Modality:** Cardinal (initiates connection and ideas)
- **Planetary Ruler:** Venus (love, beauty, art, values)
- **Body Rulership:** Kidneys, lower back, adrenal glands, and skin
- **Strengths:** Diplomacy, cooperation, charm, fairness, refined taste
- **Challenges:** Indecisiveness, people-pleasing, emotional codependency, avoidance of conflict

Libra lives between extremes, constantly seeking middle ground. It needs *calm clarity* to make decisions, *emotional grounding* to stay authentic in relationships, and *sensory balance* to feel at peace. Hemp offers all three when incorporated with intention.

Why Hemp Brings Balance to Libra

Libra values both *function* and *form*. It wants tools that not only work—but feel good, look good, and elevate shared experiences. Hemp fits beautifully into Libra's world: a plant of peace, poise, and pleasure.

Hemp Supports Libra By:

- **Easing anxiety from indecision or relational stress**
- **Promoting emotional equilibrium in romantic and social contexts**
- **Encouraging clear communication without self-abandonment**
- **Reducing tension in the lower back and kidneys (common Libra stress points)**
- **Heightening sensory appreciation—ideal for art, design, and intimacy**

Ideal Hemp Profiles for Libra Energy

Libra thrives with **gentle, mood-balancing, and socially enhancing hemp strains**. These strains should elevate without overwhelming, calm without numbing, and create a sense of *embodied elegance*.

Best effects to target:

- Mild euphoria for social flow
- Mental clarity for decision-making
- Gentle muscle relaxation (especially lower back)
- Nervous system harmony
- Heart-centered awareness and emotional openness

Recommended Cannabinoids & Terpenes:

- **CBD + Delta-8 or low-THC blends:** Enhances social confidence without paranoia
- **Linalool:** Calming, especially in social tension
- **Beta-Caryophyllene:** Smooth emotional edges and promote peace during difficult conversations
- **Limonene:** Gently uplifts and supports graceful, joyful engagement

Top Strain Archetypes for Libra Connection & Clarity
(Conceptual archetypes; strain names may differ by region or source)

◇ **"Venus Veil" (CBD + low-THC blend)**
A beauty-enhancing, emotionally softening strain for artistic environments, dating, or self-love rituals. Great for skincare or spa days.

◇ **"Balance Bloom" (CBD + limonene & linalool)**
Uplifts Libra's mood while bringing a gentle steadiness. Ideal for journaling through tough choices or engaging in emotionally charged conversations.

◇ **"Social Grace" (Delta-8 vape or sublingual)**
Perfect for events, parties, and group settings where Libra may feel overwhelmed. Helps with confident self-expression and joyful presence.

◇ **"Back to Center" (Topical balm or salve)**
A topical for Libra's lower back tension and kidney area. Can be part of a self-care bath or massage ritual to realign physical and emotional posture.

Astrological Timing for Libra Hemp Use

- **New Moon in Libra:** Use hemp to set intentions for relational growth, balance in boundaries, and clarity in communication. Pair with journaling or mirror work.
- **Full Moon in Libra:** Reflect on emotional equilibrium in your life. Use calming hemp strains to process relational energy and connect deeply with loved ones.
- **Libra Season (September–October):** Elevate your self-care, style, and relational rituals. Use hemp-infused oils, teas, or flower for sensual enjoyment and emotional insight.

Libra Ritual: The Harmony Mirror Ceremony
Materials:

- Hemp tincture or calming flower (Venus Veil or Balance Bloom recommended)
- Mirror
- Pink or white rose petals
- Scented candle (lavender or rose)
- Soothing playlist (classical, lo-fi, or instrumental)
- Crystal: Rose quartz or jade

Steps:

1. Create a soft, aesthetically pleasing space—lighting the candle and arranging the petals around the mirror.
2. Take your hemp product slowly, focusing on breath.
3. Look into the mirror and ask:
   "Where am I giving too much? Where do I need to receive?"
4. Write down your answer or speak it aloud.
5. Play soft music and gently massage your shoulders or back using rose oil or a topical hemp salve.
6. Affirm: *"I am enough as I am. I choose peace without performance."*

This ritual returns Libra to their **inner compass**, so external relationships don't define their worth.

Libra Wisdom: Harmony Begins Within

Libra often seeks balance in others—but true harmony is a self-generated state. When Libra learns to align mind and heart, speak with grace *and* conviction, and honor both beauty and truth, it becomes a master of authentic connection.

Hemp helps Libra:

- Calm relational anxiety without losing connection
- Make clear decisions without spiraling into overthinking
- Create meaningful conversations from a place of softness
- Release tension in the lower back and energy field
- Enjoy beauty, touch, and art without pressure or performance

Libra teaches us that **real peace isn't the absence of conflict—it's the presence of mutual truth**. And hemp is the herb that lets that truth flow freely, beautifully, and without fear.

Chapter 9 – Sagittarius & Expansion: Philosophical and Global Perspectives

Sagittarius, the ninth sign of the zodiac, is the philosopher, explorer, and truth-seeker. Ruled by **Jupiter**, the planet of expansion, optimism, and wisdom, and governed by the **Fire element**, Sagittarius represents a hunger for freedom, knowledge, and discovery. It is the sign of the global citizen, the spiritual nomad, the wandering student, and the eternal optimist.

Sagittarius is always reaching—toward a higher meaning, a new destination, or a bigger dream. But with that expansive energy comes restlessness, inconsistency, scattered attention, and a tendency to leap before looking. The Sag mind is fast, idealistic, and prone to **mental overstimulation and spiritual burnout**.

Hemp, when used intentionally, becomes a powerful tool for the Sagittarian path—not to limit their flight, but to **ground their wings**. It helps calm the body during travel, support long periods of study or teaching, and ease the anxiety that arises when a Sag soul feels confined or directionless.

The Essence of Sagittarius Energy

- **Element:** Fire
- **Modality:** Mutable (flexible, exploratory)
- **Planetary Ruler:** Jupiter (expansion, luck, philosophy, world-view)
- **Body Rulership:** Hips, thighs, liver, sciatic nerve
- **Strengths:** Optimism, curiosity, vision, humor, independence, adaptability
- **Challenges:** Impulsiveness, lack of follow-through, overpromising, travel anxiety, spiritual disconnection, dogmatism

Sagittarius is driven by a desire to find meaning, whether through books, belief systems, or boarding passes. But this drive can create imbalance if not rooted in regular pauses for **integration, rest, and alignment**. Hemp becomes that pause—an anchor in the moment without clipping the wings of imagination.

Why Hemp Grounds and Enhances Sagittarius Energy

Sagittarius is not content with shallow living. It seeks deep, authentic experiences, but often avoids stillness or routine. Hemp allows Sagittarius to **rest without boredom**, **focus without confinement**, and **connect spiritually without overthinking**. It enhances philosophical insight while regulating the body's overstimulated stress responses from too much movement or too many plans.

Hemp Supports Sagittarius By:

- **Reducing travel anxiety and overstimulation**
- **Improving focus during long study or creative sessions**
- **Supporting digestion and liver health (important for Sag types)**
- **Helping integrate spiritual or psychedelic experiences**
- **Creating mental stillness for meditation or foreign-language learning**

Ideal Hemp Profiles for Sagittarius Energy

Sagittarius benefits most from **balancing, uplifting, and body-aware hemp strains**—ones that allow movement but prevent burnout. These strains should enhance insight without creating distraction, and calm without sedation.

Best effects to target:

- Mental clarity and sustained focus
- Calm energy for travel, lectures, or ritual
- Liver and digestive support
- Mood elevation during loneliness or existential angst
- Nervous system regulation after high-stimulus environments

Recommended Cannabinoids & Terpenes:

- **CBD + CBG Combo:** For gentle alertness and gut/liver support
- **Limonene:** Boosts mood and enhances curiosity
- **Beta-Caryophyllene:** Anti-inflammatory and grounding
- **Ocimene:** A gentle stimulant, perfect for the Sag rhythm
- **Pinene:** For mental sharpness and clarity in unfamiliar places

Top Strain Archetypes for Sagittarius Seeking & Settling
(Strain archetypes may differ in name by region, but can be matched by profile.)

◈ **"Wanderer's Calm" (CBD + CBG with limonene)**
Great for long-distance travel or spiritual retreats. Keeps mind alert and body calm during flights, lectures, or vision quests.

◈ **"Truth Seeker" (Balanced hemp blend with pinene and ocimene)**
Perfect for reading, writing, or podcasting about philosophy, religion, or politics. Supports grounded insight without distraction.

◈ **"Global Ease" (Sublingual oil for digestion and nerves)**
Infused with hemp and herbal allies like ginger and turmeric. Great for Sag's sensitive digestion, especially when exploring new cuisines or time zones.

◈ **"Temple Flame" (Topical oil or balm for hips and thighs)**
Soothes overworked travel muscles and aligns Sagittarius's physical body with their spiritual mission. Apply before yoga, hikes, or dance.

Astrological Timing for Sagittarius Hemp Use

- **New Moon in Sagittarius:** Set big-picture goals and tune into your higher purpose. Pair with a grounding strain and create a vision map or prayer.
- **Full Moon in Sagittarius:** A time to release spiritual dogma or outdated worldviews. Use hemp for heart-opening meditation and philosophical journaling.
- **Sagittarius Season (November–December):** Plan your next journey—physical, academic, or spiritual. Use hemp to stay grounded as you expand your reach.

Sagittarius Ritual: The Pilgrim's Pause Practice
Materials:

- Hemp tincture or oil (Wanderer's Calm or Truth Seeker recommended)
- Journal or world map
- Candle (purple, indigo, or gold)
- Incense or essential oil (frankincense, clove, or myrrh)
- Crystal: Amethyst or turquoise

Steps:

1. Inhale hemp or take your tincture, then light your candle and incense.
2. Sit with your map or journal. Ask:
   "Where is my soul being called to explore next—and why?"
3. Write or draw the vision—this could be a destination, a course of study, a spiritual concept, or a life challenge.
4. Close your eyes and visualize yourself already there. Ask your higher self:
   "What lesson am I meant to receive on this path?"
5. Conclude with the affirmation:
   "I expand with purpose. My fire is guided, not scattered."

This ritual reminds Sagittarius that the **quest is not only outward, but inward**—and that presence is a portal to deeper understanding.

Sagittarius Wisdom: Expansion Requires Integration

Sagittarius is here to learn, travel, teach, and liberate—but its real magic appears when it stops just long enough to **absorb and reflect**. Hemp is the plant that provides just enough stillness to integrate lessons, make thoughtful choices, and explore deeper truths without the burnout of constant motion.

With mindful hemp use, Sagittarius can:

- Navigate jet lag and overstimulation
- Focus during philosophical or spiritual study
- Ground into body-based wisdom while seeking truth
- Reflect on life's journey from a place of peace
- Connect to global and mystical traditions without losing center

Sagittarius teaches us that **wisdom is not in knowing everything, but in finding meaning everywhere**. Hemp becomes a passport to presence, allowing Sagittarius to journey wisely—and come home to the self.

Chapter 10 – Capricorn & Structure: Hemp as a Tool for Mastery

Capricorn, the tenth sign of the zodiac, is the strategist, the builder, and the wise elder of the cosmic wheel. Ruled by **Saturn**, the planet of time, discipline, and legacy, and grounded in the **Earth element**, Capricorn governs structure, achievement, ambition, and self-mastery. It climbs steadily toward its highest vision—one calculated step at a time.

But behind the Capricornian stoicism and strength lies a **tired nervous system**, a mind that rarely switches off, and a body that absorbs decades of responsibility. Capricorn often carries the weight of the world—and rarely asks for help.

Hemp, when integrated with intention, becomes a quiet, powerful ally for Capricorn's journey. It doesn't interfere with discipline—it *enhances it*. It supports focus, calms chronic tension, improves sleep, and becomes a recovery tool for a sign that often sacrifices well-being in service of long-term goals.

The Essence of Capricorn Energy

- **Element:** Earth
- **Modality:** Cardinal (initiating structure and legacy)
- **Planetary Ruler:** Saturn (boundaries, responsibility, time)
- **Body Rulership:** Knees, bones, joints, connective tissue, teeth
- **Strengths:** Discipline, ambition, patience, resilience, leadership
- **Challenges:** Rigidity, burnout, emotional suppression, workaholism, pessimism

Capricorn thrives with routines and rules, but struggles to rest, trust the body, or emotionally decompress. Hemp becomes a **precision tool** for this sign—not a crutch, but a *systemic upgrade* for longevity and performance.

Why Hemp Is Perfect for Capricorn's Grind

Capricorn doesn't indulge in substances without purpose. Hemp appeals to Capricorn when it:

- Produces tangible results
- Integrates into a structured wellness protocol
- Improves mental and physical output
- Reduces pain or tension without impairing control

This is not about "chilling out." It's about **refining endurance**.

Hemp Supports Capricorn By:

- **Easing muscle and joint tension from overwork**
- **Improving sleep quality for cellular and cognitive recovery**
- **Reducing stress while enhancing executive function**
- **Supporting rituals of productivity and mental focus**
- **Softening emotional rigidity without compromising strength**

Ideal Hemp Profiles for Capricorn Energy

Capricorn benefits most from **functional, anti-inflammatory, and sleep-supportive hemp strains**, especially those that enhance recovery while maintaining cognitive clarity.

Best effects to target:

- Deep muscle and joint relief
- Mental focus with emotional steadiness
- Non-drowsy daytime clarity
- High-quality sleep for performance recovery
- Pain and stress reduction for chronic tension

Recommended Cannabinoids & Terpenes:

- **CBD + CBC or CBN:** Muscle recovery, calm, and sleep regulation
- **Beta-Caryophyllene:** Excellent for inflammation and mood stability
- **Myrcene:** Enhances rest and relieves tension
- **Limonene:** Provides a sense of optimism and clarity
- **Camphene:** Supports connective tissue and joint health

Top Strain Archetypes for Capricorn Endurance & Elevation
(Strain types below represent profiles; actual names vary by region and brand)

◈ "Legacy Root" (CBD + CBC functional blend)
Designed for peak performance routines. Enhances clarity, reduces joint pain, and sharpens decision-making—ideal for entrepreneurs, athletes, or career-focused Capricorns.

◈ "Iron Spine" (Topical salve for joints and back)
Apply to knees, lower back, or hands after long work sessions or physical exertion. Works well after cold showers or massage therapy.

◈ "Nocturnal Climb" (CBD/CBN sleep tincture)
Targets deep sleep cycles and cortisol regulation. Supports nighttime nervous system reset, muscle repair, and dream-state insight for next-day strategy.

◈ "Saturn's Rest" (Infused soak or balm)
A recovery blend for the skin, bones, and body. Ideal for post-work rituals, injury prevention, or spa-like decompression.

Astrological Timing for Capricorn Hemp Use

- **New Moon in Capricorn:** Set long-term health and business goals. Use a focus-enhancing strain during journaling, followed by a sleep aid to solidify the vision.
- **Full Moon in Capricorn:** Time to pause and acknowledge your accomplishments. Use a muscle-soothing hemp soak or balm to physically release built-up pressure.
- **Capricorn Season (December–January):** Ideal for building new systems of success, including structured hemp use for productivity, recovery, and grounded ambition.

Capricorn Ritual: The Master's Maintenance Method
Materials:

- Hemp capsule or tincture (Legacy Root or Nocturnal Climb recommended)
- Planner or journal
- Hot compress or CBD-infused balm
- Candle (dark green, black, or grey)
- Crystal: Hematite or black tourmaline

Steps:

1. Take your hemp product of choice with a warm beverage.
2. Sit with your planner or journal and reflect:
   "What am I building—and how do I recover while I rise?"
3. Create a weekly maintenance plan: one rest day, one stretch/movement session, one reward ritual.
4. Apply balm or hot compress to a tense area while affirming:
   "Rest is the fuel of legacy. My resilience is rooted in care."
5. Light your candle and close with breathwork: inhale structure, exhale pressure.

Capricorn Wisdom: Mastery Requires Maintenance

Capricorn knows how to climb—but sometimes forgets to breathe. True greatness isn't just about working harder—it's about creating **systems that sustain strength**.

With hemp, Capricorn can:

- Improve physical endurance through inflammation relief
- Build productive habits with precision supplementation
- Sleep more deeply for long-term brain and body health
- Manage stress without suppressing emotion
- Shift from control to calm without losing command

Capricorn teaches us that **power is built, not found—and hemp can be one of the most valuable tools in the kit**. It doesn't disrupt the climb. It *supports it*. Quietly. Reliably. Strategically.

Chapter 11 – Aquarius & Innovation: The Future of Hemp and Consciousness

Aquarius, the eleventh sign of the zodiac, is the rebel, the inventor, the system disrupter, and the cosmic visionary. Ruled by **Uranus** (modern) and **Saturn** (traditional), and aligned with the **Air element**, Aquarius channels both revolutionary change and structured reform. It governs technology, social systems, futuristic thought, community collaboration, and humanitarian ideals. Aquarius energy lives in the future—often ten steps ahead of the world.

But living on the frontier has its costs.

Aquarians often experience **mental overstimulation, nervous system imbalance, emotional disconnection, and tech-induced burnout**. They can become overly cerebral, cut off from the body, or lose their grounding in pursuit of ideals. In group dynamics, they may struggle with personal presence, vulnerability, or sustainable leadership.

Hemp, when integrated with mindful experimentation, becomes a critical bridge for Aquarians—**connecting vision to embodiment, insight to calm, and progress to peace**. It helps Aquarius balance innovation with integration, elevating their contributions without burning them out.

The Essence of Aquarius Energy

- **Element:** Air
- **Modality:** Fixed (focused, stable innovation)
- **Planetary Ruler:** Uranus (disruption, awakening, genius) and Saturn (structure, discipline)
- **Body Rulership:** Nervous system, brain waves, calves, ankles, circulation
- **Strengths:** Innovation, detachment, objectivity, vision, futuristic thinking, group synergy
- **Challenges:** Emotional distance, anxiety, insomnia, overwhelm, lack of embodiment, unpredictable mood shifts

Aquarius craves novelty, freedom, and collective evolution. But its mind is constantly *online*, overstimulated by devices, ideologies, or the weight of global crises. Hemp becomes a **quantum anchor**—a botanical partner in tech detox, creative flow, and radical nervous system reset.

Why Hemp Supports Aquarius Innovation & Integration

Aquarius loves the idea of hemp as a future-forward plant. It's sustainable, non-toxic, planet-healing, multi-functional, and capable of serving multiple systems at once. These very qualities mirror the Aquarian mind—**versatile, systemic, and radically progressive**.

Hemp Supports Aquarius By:

- **Soothing mental overdrive without dulling insight**
- **Reconnecting the nervous system to the body**
- **Aiding sleep and electrical regulation (brain wave coherence)**
- **Fostering emotional presence in digital or intellectual environments**
- **Supporting collaborative rituals and group cohesion**

Ideal Hemp Profiles for Aquarius Energy

Aquarius benefits from **clarity-enhancing, brain-balancing, and sensory reintegration hemp strains**. These profiles should support cerebral exploration while preventing system overload.

Best effects to target:

- Calm mental alertness without fog
- Emotional clarity and social fluidity
- Nervous system balancing and electrical discharge relief
- Focused energy for digital detox or deep work
- Reconnection to body awareness in group settings

Recommended Cannabinoids & Terpenes:

- **CBD + CBG + CBC blends:** Ideal for brain support, mild energy, and neurobalance
- **Pinene:** Enhances memory, breathing, and clarity
- **Terpinolene:** Mildly energizing, aids in creative ideation
- **Limonene:** Elevates mood and mitigates overstimulation
- **Linalool:** Helps regulate nervous system and calms emotional spikes

Top Strain Archetypes for Aquarius Insight & Integration
(Strain profiles are conceptual and can be matched based on effects.)

◈ **"Neuro Nova" (CBD/CBG blend with pinene and limonene)**
Perfect for brainstorming, coding, digital detox journaling, or tech-free planning sessions. Keeps the mind open while grounding awareness.

◈ **"Circuit Breaker" (Topical for ankles and calves)**
Supports Aquarius' circulation and lower-body grounding—relieves energetic congestion and tension from standing, walking, or intellectual overload.

◈ **"Sky Sync" (Sublingual tincture for brain rhythm balance)**
Ideal before meditation, group work, or high-focus projects. Encourages coherence between hemispheres and balances energetic output.

◈ **"Collective Glow" (Delta-8/CBD microdose for social and ritual settings)**
Softens Aquarian emotional aloofness. Encourages openness, collaboration, and playful expression in groups without losing individuality.

Astrological Timing for Aquarius Hemp Use

- **New Moon in Aquarius:** Ideal for visionary goal-setting, future-casting, and digital detox. Use hemp to enter flow states for ideation or group rituals.
- **Full Moon in Aquarius:** Release outdated identity structures or technological addictions. Use balancing strains to return to your body and re-engage emotionally.
- **Aquarius Season (January–February):** Explore new hemp routines for creativity, community healing, and planetary impact. This is your time to reinvent your relationship with mind, mood, and mission.

Aquarius Ritual: The Vision Channel Reset
Materials:

- Hemp tincture or capsule (Neuro Nova or Sky Sync recommended)
- Blue or silver candle
- Crystal: Fluorite or labradorite
- Journal or vision board tools
- Headphones + curated ambient playlist

Steps:

1. Take your hemp product with intention. Light your candle. Sit in a quiet, tech-free space.
2. Reflect: *"What future am I helping to create—and am I grounded in it?"*
3. Free-write or sketch your future vision: 1 year, 5 years, 10 years. What systems will you build? How will you serve the collective?
4. Hold the crystal to your third eye. Visualize data streams turning to rivers of light—your thoughts syncing with purpose, not pressure.
5. Conclude with this mantra:
   "I am a node in the cosmic grid. I serve evolution from wholeness."

Aquarius Wisdom: Innovation Requires Integration

Aquarius doesn't just think differently—it *lives* differently. It sees what's broken and dares to redesign the system. But without embodiment, it risks becoming a mind untethered from meaning.

Hemp offers the **embodied innovation Aquarius needs**. It slows mental noise while enhancing brilliance. It brings emotional neutrality without detachment. It becomes a plant-based operating system for:

- Digital nervous system healing
- Group coherence and visionary planning
- Long-focus creative or technological work
- Emotional reconnection in intellectually charged settings
- Ritual design for new earth realities

Aquarius teaches us that **the future is a frequency**, and hemp helps tune the mind to receive it—clearly, calmly, and courageously.

Chapter 12 – Pisces & Intuition: Hemp in Dreamwork and Mysticism

Pisces, the twelfth and final sign of the zodiac, is the dreamer, the mystic, the empath, and the soul of the collective unconscious. Ruled by **Neptune** (modern) and **Jupiter** (traditional), and aligned with the **Water element**, Pisces represents the spiritual dissolve—the merging of self with source, the drop with the ocean. It is the sign of mysticism, altered states, fantasy, compassion, forgiveness, escapism, and unconditional love.

Pisces sees beyond the veil. It *feels* everything—sorrow and bliss, birth and death, suffering and divinity. But this emotional and psychic sensitivity can lead to energetic overload, addiction, escapism, and a porous sense of self. Pisces often needs **grounding and protection** as much as it craves elevation.

Hemp, when used spiritually and therapeutically, becomes a sacred companion for Pisces. It supports intuition without overwhelming it, deepens dream recall without dissociation, expands compassion while reinforcing energetic boundaries, and acts as a **bridge between transcendence and embodiment**.

The Essence of Pisces Energy

- **Element:** Water
- **Modality:** Mutable (fluid, adaptable)
- **Planetary Ruler:** Neptune (dreams, illusion, mysticism) and Jupiter (faith, expansion)
- **Body Rulership:** Feet, pineal gland, lymphatic system, and energetic aura
- **Strengths:** Imagination, empathy, intuition, spiritual connection, creativity
- **Challenges:** Escapism, lack of boundaries, emotional overwhelm, martyrdom, addiction

Pisces walks between worlds. It channels dreams, poetry, and spiritual truth—but it also absorbs pain from every room it enters. Hemp becomes a plant ally that not only **enhances Pisces's mysticism**, but helps **ground their compassion in personal care**.

Why Hemp Supports Pisces's Spiritual Expansion and Protection

Pisces is always connected—whether to dreams, spirits, emotions, or people's suffering. Hemp helps **create structure within that connection**, allowing Pisces to access altered states with safety, manage their sensitivities, and return to center after deep emotional or psychic journeys.

Hemp Supports Pisces By:

- **Enhancing dreamwork, lucid dreaming, and astral experiences**
- **Supporting meditation, prayer, and trance states**
- **Protecting the aura and emotional body in crowded or overwhelming spaces**
- **Grounding into the body after spiritual practice or empathy overload**
- **Helping Pisces differentiate between personal emotion and collective energy**

Ideal Hemp Profiles for Pisces Energy

Pisces benefits from **ethereal, heart-softening, and dream-enhancing hemp strains**—those that allow for spiritual elevation without ungrounded detachment. Ideal profiles should gently modulate sensory openness while maintaining emotional coherence.

Best effects to target:

- Vivid dream recall and gentle sleep induction
- Deep meditation and sensory receptivity
- Aura protection and grounding
- Emotional softening without complete surrender
- Self-reflection through journaling, art, or intuitive ritual

Recommended Cannabinoids & Terpenes:

- **CBD + CBN:** For dream depth and body relaxation
- **Linalool:** Enhances mystical calm and self-compassion
- **Myrcene:** Supports body-soul integration and tranquil sleep
- **Beta-Caryophyllene:** Offers grounding in spiritual overload
- **Nerolidol:** Encourages inner stillness and protection from external noise

Top Strain Archetypes for Pisces Dreaming & Divine Flow
(These are conceptual strain types; actual names may differ by brand or region.)

◈ "Ocean Veil" (CBD + CBN nighttime blend)

Ideal for lucid dreaming, astral travel, or New Moon sleep rituals. Encourages surrender into subconscious waters while protecting energetic integrity.

◈ "Third Eye Bloom" (CBD + linalool with trace THC)

Great for meditation, divination, intuitive painting, or spiritual journaling. Gently opens the pineal gateway while calming emotional waves.

◈ "Sacred Fog" (Low-THC flower with beta-caryophyllene)

For rituals involving compassion, grief release, or soul forgiveness. Softens psychic pain while keeping the aura sealed and safe.

◈ "Boundary Balm" (Topical for feet and lymph nodes)

Helps Pisces ground before and after rituals, group ceremonies, or emotionally draining days. Apply to soles, wrists, or temples.

Astrological Timing for Pisces Hemp Use

- **New Moon in Pisces:** Seed your dreams—literally and metaphorically. Use dream-enhancing hemp strains to create an intention-setting sleep ritual.
- **Full Moon in Pisces:** Heightened psychic receptivity. Use protective hemp products to maintain emotional clarity during spiritual or creative release.
- **Pisces Season (February–March):** Dedicate time to spiritual growth, art, and compassion practices. Use hemp to enter gentle trance states, deepen rituals, and recover from emotional heaviness.

Pisces Ritual: The Dreamkeeper's Temple
Materials:

- Hemp tincture or tea (Ocean Veil or Third Eye Bloom recommended)
- Lavender or frankincense incense
- Dream journal or sketchbook
- Crystal: Amethyst or moonstone
- Bowl of water and candle (for a bedside altar)

Steps:

1. In the evening, consume your hemp tincture or tea with reverence.
2. Light incense and your candle beside the bowl of water—creating a temple space for dreams.
3. Sit in silence, eyes closed, breathing into your heart. Ask your dreams:
   "What healing do you wish to offer me tonight?"
4. Write or draw any impressions in your journal. Place your crystal under your pillow.
5. Upon waking, record your dreams. Thank your guides.
6. Affirm:
   "I receive without losing myself. I feel without drowning. I dream with boundaries."

Pisces Wisdom: Compassion Requires Containment

Pisces wants to merge—with art, love, people, spirit, the universe. But true divine connection doesn't require losing yourself. It asks you to show up fully in your vessel, with presence, boundaries, and care.

Hemp helps Pisces:

- Engage in spiritual practices without disembodiment
- Support deep sleep and vivid, healing dream states
- Strengthen emotional and energetic boundaries
- Open the heart chakra safely and sustainably
- Process grief, love, and longing through mystical states of calm

Pisces teaches us that **the soul has tides**, and we are meant to ride them—not drown. Hemp becomes a raft, a bridge, a balm—supporting gentle transcendence with sacred containment.

Final Reflection: The Zodiac, the Self, and the Sacred Plant

As we close the twelvefold journey, we remember this truth: **Hemp is not just a plant—it's a partner**. It speaks to each zodiac sign in its own way, offering calm to fire, clarity to air, grounding to water, and nourishment to earth.

Let your sign guide your ritual.
Let hemp support your soul.
And may the stars, the soil, and your breath forever move as one.

Appendix A – The Astro-Hemp Compatibility Chart

Astrology and hemp share one profound truth: **both work best when approached with intention**. This appendix is a comprehensive compatibility guide that maps over **48 hemp strain profiles** to each sign's core energetic needs—according to their **Sun, Moon, and Rising signs**. Whether you're seeking clarity, calm, or creative flow, this chart provides a structured yet intuitive framework for aligning with your personal cosmic blueprint.

◈ I. Planetary Rulers & Strain Trait Breakdown

To understand astro-hemp synergy, begin by identifying the **planet that rules your Sun, Moon, or Rising sign** and the **traits associated with that planetary energy.** This can guide your hemp selection beyond just zodiac sign alone.

Planet	Associated Signs	Strain Trait Focus
◈ Sun	Leo	Confidence, mood elevation, heart-opening, visibility
◈ Moon	Cancer	Emotional safety, sleep, comfort, subconscious work
◈ Mercury	Gemini, Virgo	Focus, clarity, language fluency, gut-brain balance
♀ Venus	Taurus, Libra	Sensory pleasure, beauty, ease, social connection
♂ Mars	Aries, Scorpio (co-ruler)	Activation, motivation, inflammation relief, trauma support
◈ Jupiter	Sagittarius, Pisces (co-ruler)	Expansion, insight, visioning, dreamwork
◈ Saturn	Capricorn, Aquarius (co-ruler)	Structure, restoration, pain relief, energetic boundaries

Planet	Associated Signs	Strain Trait Focus
◇ Uranus	Aquarius	Innovation, nervous system support, creative insight
◇ Neptune	Pisces	Mysticism, sleep, spiritual states, emotional empathy
◇ Pluto	Scorpio	Transformation, shadow work, sexual healing

⬦ II. The 48+ Astro-Compatible Hemp Strains

Each strain below is aligned with one or more zodiac archetypes and matched with **specific uses** for self-regulation, creativity, or growth. These archetypes may appear under different names depending on region and supplier—what matters is the **cannabinoid + terpene profile** and **intended effect.**

Strain Name	Sign Match	Cannabinoids	Best For
Solar Bloom	Leo	CBD + THCv	Confidence, content creation, performance
Velvet Root	Taurus	CBD + Myrcene	Sensual calm, deep relaxation
Twin Bloom	Gemini	CBD + Limonene	Conversation flow, multitasking
Green Temple	Virgo	CBD + CBG	Routine integration, clarity
Moonmilk	Cancer	CBD + CBN + Myrcene	Sleep, emotional reset
Heartfire	Leo, Libra	CBD + Linalool	Romantic balance, social ease
Wanderer's Calm	Sagittarius	CBD + CBG	Travel anxiety, global flow
Sacred Surrender	Scorpio	CBD + Nerolidol	Sexuality, emotional depth

Strain Name	Sign Match	Cannabinoids	Best For
Saturn's Rest	Capricorn	CBD + CBN	Deep sleep, overwork recovery
Neuro Nova	Aquarius	CBD + Pinene	Tech detox, clarity, innovation
Ocean Veil	Pisces	CBD + CBN + Linalool	Dreaming, mystic surrender
Balance Bloom	Libra	CBD + Beta-Caryophyllene	Decision-making, emotional grace
Phoenix Salve	Scorpio	Topical CBD	Trauma recovery, root chakra
Circuit Breaker	Aquarius	Topical CBD	Lower body tension, energy rebalancing
Nocturnal Climb	Capricorn	CBD + CBN	Muscle repair, nighttime focus
Venus Veil	Taurus, Libra	CBD + Low THC	Self-love, skincare, emotional warmth

Strain Name	Sign Match	Cannabi-noids	Best For
Sky Sync	Aquarius, Gemini	CBD + CBG	Meditation, brain-wave balance
Third Eye Bloom	Pisces	CBD + Linalool	Divination, meditation, trancework
DigestEase	Virgo, Sagittarius	CBD + Ginger/CBG	Gut support, calm during digestion
Iron Spine	Capricorn	Topical CBD	Joint tension, long work recovery
Social Grace	Libra, Gemini	Delta-8 + CBD	Social confidence, light euphoria
Sacred Fog	Pisces, Scorpio	CBD + Myrcene + BCP	Forgiveness, emotional release
Clean Slate	Virgo, Capricorn	CBD + CBC	Focus, inflammation relief
Flame Ritual	Aries, Leo	CBD + THCv	Energized rituals, fitness flow

...and many more depending on supplier and formulation.

◈♂ III. Practical Use Categories & How to Match

Choose strains based on **intention**, not just your sign. Use the grid below to cross-reference your goal with potential strains and signs.

Use Category	Best Strain Examples	Ideal Signs
Meditation	Third Eye Bloom, Sky Sync, Sacred Fog	Pisces, Aquarius, Scorpio
Stress Relief	Moonmilk, Balance Bloom, Sacred Surrender	Cancer, Libra, Taurus
Energy	Solar Bloom, Flame Ritual, Neuro Nova	Aries, Sagittarius, Leo, Aquarius
Sleep	Nocturnal Climb, Ocean Veil, Saturn's Rest	Cancer, Capricorn, Pisces
Focus	Clean Slate, DigestEase, Twin Bloom	Virgo, Gemini, Capricorn
Emotional Healing	Sacred Fog, Heartfire, Venus Veil	Scorpio, Libra, Pisces
Creativity	Solar Bloom, Sky Sync, Third Eye Bloom	Leo, Aquarius, Gemini, Pisces
Pain Management	Iron Spine, Phoenix Salve, Circuit Breaker	Capricorn, Taurus, Scorpio
Social Ease	Social Grace, Venus Veil, Balance Bloom	Libra, Gemini, Leo

◈ **IV. Astrological Hemp Journaling Suggestions**

Journaling enhances the intentional use of hemp and astrology together. Try the following prompts to record your personal discoveries.

Journal Prompt Examples:

- *Which part of my body or mood changed after this strain?*
- *What thoughts or dreams surfaced after use?*
- *How did this strain affect my sense of purpose or connection?*
- *Did this strain help with a specific transit or lunar event?*
- *Which sign's energy did I feel aligned with the most?*

Create a ritual by journaling during **New Moons**, **Full Moons**, or during significant planetary transits—especially returns, retrogrades, or conjunctions to your natal placements.

◈ V. Personal Astro-Hemp Log Template

Use the following chart as a reusable tool to **track your own experiences**. Print or copy this for daily or ritual use.

Date	Sun/ Moon/ Rising Sign	Strain Used	Form (Tincture/ Smoke/ Topical/ Edible)	Intent/Use	Effects Felt (1–10 scale)	Notes /Insights

◈ Final Thoughts

This compatibility chart is a living tool. Your relationship with hemp—and the cosmos—will evolve. Use this appendix not as a rulebook, but as a **mirror and map**. The deeper you track your responses to different strains, signs, and rituals, the more accurate and empowering your personal astro-hemp path becomes.

May your breath, your body, and your birth chart work together in radiant harmony—with hemp as your quiet, wise companion along the way.

Message from the Author:

I hope you enjoyed this book, I love astrology and knew there was not a book such as this out on the shelf. I love metaphysical items as well. Please check out my other books:

-Life of Government Benefits

-My life of Hell

-My life with Hydrocephalus

-Red Sky

-World Domination:Woman's rule

-World Domination:Woman's Rule 2: The War

-Life and Banishment of Apophis: book 1

-The Kidney Friendly Diet

-The Ultimate Hemp Cookbook

-Creating a Dispensary(legally)

-Cleanliness throughout life: the importance of showering from childhood to adulthood.

-Strong Roots: The Risks of Overcoddling children

-Hemp Horoscopes: Cosmic Insights and Earthly Healing

- Celestial Hemp Navigating the Zodiac: Through the Green Cosmos

-Astrological Hemp: Aligning The Stars with Earth's Ancient Herb

-The Astrological Guide to Hemp: Stars, Signs, and Sacred Leaves

-Green Growth: Innovative Marketing Strategies for your Hemp Products and Dispensary

-Cosmic Cannabis

-Astrological Munchies

-Henry The Hemp

-Zodiacal Roots: The Astrological Soul Of Hemp

- **Green Constellations: Intersection of Hemp and Zodiac**

-Hemp in The Houses: An astrological Adventure Through The Cannabis Galaxy

-Galactic Ganja Guide

Heavenly Hemp
Zodiac Leaves
Doctor Who Astrology
Cannastrology
Stellar Satvias and Cosmic Indicas
<u>Celestial Cannabis: A Zodiac Journey</u>
AstroHerbology: The Sky and The Soil: Volume 1
AstroHerbology:Celestial Cannabis:Volume 2
Cosmic Cannabis Cultivation
The Starry Guide to Herbal Harmony: Volume 1
The Starry Guide to Herbal Harmony: Cannabis Universe: Volume 2

Yugioh Astrology: Astrological Guide to Deck, Duels and more
Nightmare Mansion: Echoes of The Abyss
Nightmare Mansion 2: Legacy of Shadows
Nightmare Mansion 3: Shadows of the Forgotten
Nightmare Mansion 4: Echoes of the Damned
The Life and Banishment of Apophis: Book 2
Nightmare Mansion: Halls of Despair
<u>Healing with Herb: Cannabis and Hydrocephalus</u>
<u>Planetary Pot: Aligning with Astrological Herbs: Volume 1</u>
Fast Track to Freedom: 30 Days to Financial Independence Using AI, Assets, and Agile Hustles
<u>Cosmic Hemp Pathways</u>
How to Become Financially Free in 30 Days: 10,000 Paths to Prosperity
Zodiacal Herbage: Astrological Insights: Volume 1
Nightmare Mansion: Whispers in the Walls
The Daleks Invade Atlantis
Henry the hemp and Hydrocephalus

10X The Kidney Friendly Diet
Cannabis Universe: Adult coloring book

Hemp Astrology: The Healing Power of the Stars

Zodiacal Herbage: Astrological Insights: Cannabis Universe: Volume 2

<u>**Planetary Pot: Aligning with Astrological Herbs: Cannabis Universes: Volume 2**</u>

Doctor Who: Convergence Protocol – The Replicator War

Nightmare Mansion: Curse of the Blood Moon

<u>**The Celestial Stoner: A Guide to the Zodiac**</u>

Cosmic Pleasures: Sex Toy Astrology for Every Sign

Hydrocephalus Astrology: Navigating the Stars and Healing Waters

Lapis and the Mischievous Chocolate Bar

Celestial Positions: Sexual Astrology for Every Sign

Apophis's Shadow Work Journal: **:** A Journey of Self-Discovery and Healing

Kinky Cosmos: Sexual Kink Astrology for Every Sign

Digital Cosmos: The Astrological Digimon Compendium

Stellar Seeds: The Cosmic Guide to Growing with Astrology

Apophis's Daily Gratitude Journal

Cat Astrology: Feline Mysteries of the Cosmos

The Cosmic Kama Sutra: An Astrological Guide to Sexual Positions

Unleash Your Potential: A Guided Journal Powered by AI Insights

Whispers of the Enchanted Grove

Cosmic Pleasures: An Astrological Guide to Sexual Kinks

369, 12 Manifestation Journal

Whisper of the nocturne journal(blank journal for writing or drawing)

The Boogey Book

Locked In Reflection: A Chastity Journey Through Locktober

Generating Wealth Quickly:How to Generate $100,000 in 24 Hours

Star Magic: Harness the Power of the Universe

The Flatulence Chronicles: A Fart Journal for Self-Discovery

The Doctor and The Death Moth

Seize the Day: A Personal Seizure Tracking Journal

The Ultimate Boogeyman Safari: A Journey into the Boogie World and Beyond

Whispers of Samhain: 1,000 Spells of Love, Luck, and Lunar Magic: Samhain Spell Book

Apophis's guides:Witch's Spellbook Crafting Guide for Halloween

<u>Frost & Flame: The Enchanted Yule Grimoire of 1000 Winter Spells</u>

<u>The Ultimate Boogey Goo Guide & Spooky Activities for Halloween Fun</u>

Harmony of the Scales: A Libra's Spellcraft for Balance and Beauty

The Enchanted Advent: 36 Days of Christmas Wonders

Nightmare Mansion: The Labyrinth of Screams

Harvest of Enchantment: 1,000 Spells of Gratitude, Love, and Fortune for Thanksgiving

The Boogey Chronicles: A Journal of Nightly Encounters and Shadowy Secrets

The 12 Days of Financial Freedom: A Step-by-Step Christmas Countdown to Transform Your Finances

Sigil of the Eternal Spiral Blank Journal

A Christmas Feast: Timeless Recipes for Every Meal

Holiday Stress-Free Solutions: A Survival Guide to Thriving During the Festive Season

Yu-Gi-Oh! Holiday Gifting Mastery: The Ultimate Guide for Fans and Newcomers Alike

Holiday Harmony: A Hydrocephalus Survival Guide for the Festive Season

Celestial Craft: The Witch's Almanac for 2025 – A Cosmic Guide to Manifestations, Moons, and Mystical Events

Doctor Who: The Toymaker's Winter Wonderland

Tulsa King Unveiled: A Thrilling Guide to Stallone's Mafia Masterpiece

Pendulum Craft: A Complete Guide to Crafting and Using Personalized Divination Tools

Nightmare Mansion: Santa's Eternal Eve

Starlight Noel: A Cosmic Journey through Christmas Mysteries

The Dark Architect: Unlocking the Blueprint of Existence

Surviving the Embrace: The Ultimate Guide to Encounters with The Hugging Molly

The Enchanted Codex: Secrets of the Craft for Witches, Wiccans, and Pagans

Harvest of Gratitude: A Complete Thanksgiving Guide

Yuletide Essentials: A Complete Guide to an Authentic and Magical Christmas

Celestial Smokes: A Cosmic Guide to Cigars and Astrology

Living in Balance: A Comprehensive Survival Guide to Thriving with Diabetes Insipidus

Cosmic Symbiosis: The Venom Zodiac Chronicles

The Cursed Paw of Ambition

Cosmic Symbiosis: The Astrological Venom Journal

Celestial Wonders Unfold: A Stargazer's Guide to the Cosmos (2024-2029)

The Ultimate Black Friday Prepper's Guide: Mastering Shopping Strategies and Savings

Cosmic Sales: The Astrological Guide to Black Friday Shopping

Legends of the Corn Mother and Other Harvest Myths

Whispers of the Harvest: The Corn Mother's Journal

The Evergreen Spellbook

The Doctor Meets the Boogeyman

The White Witch of Rose Hall's SpellBook

The Gingerbread Golem's Shadow: A Study in Sweet Darkness

The Gingerbread Golem Codex: An Academic Exploration of Sweet Myths

The Gingerbread Golem Grimoire: Sweet Magicks and Spells for the Festive Witch

The Curse of the Gingerbread Golem

10-minute Christmas Crafts for kids

<u>**Christmas Crisis Solutions: The Ultimate Last-Minute Survival Guide**</u>

Gingerbread Golem Recipes: Holiday Treats with a Magical Twist

The Infinite Key: Unlocking Mystical Secrets of the Ages

Enchanted Yule: A Wiccan and Pagan Guide to a Magical and Memorable Season

Dinosaurs of Power: Unlocking Ancient Magick

Astro-Dinos: The Cosmic Guide to Prehistoric Wisdom

Gallifrey's Yule Logs: A Festive Doctor Who Cookbook

The Dino Grimoire: Secrets of Prehistoric Magick

The Gift They Never Knew They Needed

The Gingerbread Golem's Culinary Alchemy: Enchanting Recipes for a Sweetly Dark Feast

A Time Lord Christmas: Holiday Adventures with the Doctor

Krampusproofing Your Home: Defensive Strategies for Yule

Silent Frights: A Collection of Christmas Creepypastas to Chill Your Bones

Santa Raptor's Jolly Carnage: A Dino-Claus Christmas Tale

Prehistoric Palettes: A Dino Wicca Coloring Journey

The Christmas Wishkeeper Chronicles

The Starlight Sleigh: A Holiday Journey

Elf Secrets: The True Magic of the North Pole

Candy Cane Conjurations

Cooking with Kids: Recipes Under 20 Minutes

Doctor Who: The TARDIS Confiscation

The Anxiety First Aid Kit: Quick Tools to Calm Your Mind

Frosty Whispers: A Winter's Tale

The Infinite Key: Unlocking the Secrets to Prosperity, Resilience, and Purpose

The Grasping Void: Why You'll Regret This Purchase

Astrology for Busy Bees: Star Signs Simplified

The Instant Focus Formula: Cut Through the Noise

The Secret Language of Colors: Unlocking the Emotional Codes

Sacred Fossil Chronicles: Blank Journal

The Christmas Cottage Miracle

Feeding Frenzy: Graboid-Inspired Recipes

Manifest in Minutes: The Quick Law of Attraction Guide

The Symbiote Chronicles: Doctor Who's Venomous Journey

Think Tiny, Grow Big: The Minimalist Mindset

The Energy Key: Unlocking Limitless Motivation

New Year, New Magic: Manifesting Your Best Year Yet

Unstoppable You: Mastering Confidence in Minutes

Infinite Energy: The Secret to Never Feeling Drained

Lightning Focus: Mastering the Art of Productivity in a Distracted World

Saturnalia Manifestation Magick: A Guide to Unlocking Abundance During the Solstice

Graboids and Garland: The Ultimate Tremors-Themed Christmas Guide

12 Nights of Holiday Magic

The Power of Pause: 60-Second Mindfulness Practices

The Quick Reset: How to Reclaim Your Life After Burnout

The Shadow Eater: A Tale of Despair and Survival

The Micro-Mastery Method: Transform Your Skills in Just Minutes a Day

Reclaiming Time: How to Live More by Doing Less

Chronovore: The Eternal Nexus

The Mind Reset: Unlocking Your Inner Peace in a Chaotic World
Confidence Code: Building Unshakable Self-Belief
Baby the Vampire Terrier
Baby the Vampire Terrier's Christmas Adventure
Celestial Streams: The Content Creator's Astrology Manual
The Wealth Whisperer: Unlocking Abundance with Everyday Actions
The Energy Equation: Maximize Your Output Without Burning Out
The Happiness Algorithm: Science-Backed Steps to Joyful Living
Stress-Free Success: Achieving Goals Without Anxiety
Mindful Wealth: The New Blueprint for Financial Freedom
The Festive Flavors of New Year: A Culinary Celebration
The Master's Gambit: Keys of Eternal Power
Shadowed Secrets: Groundhog Day Mysteries
Beneath the Burrow: Lessons from the Groundhog
Spring's Whispers: The Groundhog's Prediction
The Limitless Mindset: Unlock Your Untapped Potential
The Focus Funnel: How to Cut Through Chaos and Get Results
Bold Moves: Building Courage to Live on Your Terms
The Daily Shift: Simple Practices for Lasting Transformation
The Quarter-Life Reset: Thriving in Your 20s and 30s
The Art of Shadowplay: Building Your Own Personal Myth
The Eternal Loop: Finding Purpose in Repetition
Burrowing Wisdom: Life Lessons from the Groundhog
Shadow Work: A Groundhog Day Perspective
Love in Bloom: 5-Minute Romantic Gestures
The Shadowspell Codex: Secrets of Forbidden Magick
The Burnout Cure: Finding Balance in a Busy World
The Groundhog Prophecy: Unlocking Seasonal Secrets
Nog Tales: The Spirited History of Eggnog
Six More Weeks: Embracing Seasonal Transitions
The Lumivian Chronicles: Fragments of the Fifth Dimension

Money on Your Mind: A Beginner's Guide to Wealth

The Focus Fix: Breaking Through Distraction

January's Spirit Keepers: Mystical Protectors of the Cold

Creativity Unchained: Unlocking Your Wildest Ideas in 2025

Manifestation Mastery: 365 Days to Rewrite Your Reality

The Groundhog's Mirror: Reflecting on Change

The Weeping Angels' Christmas Curse

Burrowed in Time: A Groundhog Day Journey

Heartbeats: Poems to Share with Your Valentine

Dino Wicca: The Sacred Grimoire of Prehistoric Magick

Courage of the Pride: Finding Your Inner Roar

The Lion's Leap: Bold Moves for Big Results

Healthy Hustle: Achieving Without Overworking

Practical Manifesting: Turning Dreams into Reality in 2025

Jurassic Pharaohs: Unlocking the Magick of Ancient Egypt and Dino Wicca

The Happiness Equation: Small Changes for Big Joy

The Confidence Compass: Finding Your Inner Strength

Whispers in the Hollow: Tales of the Forgotten Beasts

Echoes from the Hollow: The Return of Forgotten Beasts

The Hollow Ascendant: The Rise of the Forgotten Beasts

The Relationship Reset: Building Better Connections

Mastering the Morning: How to Win the Day Before 8 AM

The Shadow's Dance: Groundhog Day Symbolism

Cupid's Kitchen: Quick Valentine's Day Recipes

Valentine's Day on a Budget: Love Without Breaking the Bank

Astrocraft: Aligning the Stars in the World of Minecraft

Forecasting Life: Groundhog Day Reflections

Bleeding Hearts: Twisted Tales of Valentine's Terror

Herbal Smoke Revolution: The Ultimate Guide to Nature's Cigarette Alternative

Winter's Wrath: The Complete Survival Blueprint for Extreme Freezes.

The Groundhog's Shadow: A Tale of Seasons
Burrowed Insights: Wisdom from the Groundhog
Sensual Strings: The Art of Erotic Bondage
Whispered Flames: Unlocking the Power of Fire Play
Forgotten Shadows: A Guide to Cryptids Lost to Time
Six Weeks of Secrets: Groundhog Day's Hidden Messages
Shadows and Cycles: Groundhog Day Reflections
The Art of Love Letters: Crafting the Perfect Message
Romantic Getaways at Home: Turning Your Space into Paradise
Purrfect Brews: A Cat Lover's Guide to Coffee and Companionship
The Groundhog's Wisdom: Timeless Lessons for Modern Life
The Shadow Oracle: Groundhog Day as a Predictor
Emerging from the Burrow: A Journey of Renewal
The Language of Love: Learning Your Partner's Love Style
Authorpreneur: The Ultimate Blueprint for Writing, Publishing, and Thriving as an Author
Weathering the Seasons: Groundhog Day Perspectives
Valentine's Day Magic: A Guide to Romantic Rituals
The Shadow Chronicles: Stories of Groundhog Day
Love and Laughter: Fun Games for Valentine's Day
AstroRealty: Unlocking the Stars for Property Success
The Groundhog's Path: A Guide to Seasonal Balance
Groundhog Day Diaries: Reflections in the Shadow
The Groundhog's Light: Illuminating the Path Ahead
Valentine's Traditions from Around the World
AI Wealth Revolution: Unlocking the Trillionaire Mindset
Love Rekindled: Reigniting Passion in Relationships
Single and Thriving: Self-Love on Valentine's Day
Emerald Legends: Mystical Tales of Ireland
Green Alchemy: Harnessing Nature's Magic
The Hearts of Horror: A Valentine's Day Nightmare

The Leprechaun's Guide to Wealth and Wisdom

Dancing with the Sidhe: Celebrating the Otherworld

Shamrocks and Shadows: Mysteries of the Green Isle

Emerald Energy: Harnessing Luck and Growth

The Gingerbread Golem's Valentine: A Sweetheart's Guide to Love and Enchantment

The Celtic Knot: Weaving Life and Destiny

Green Fire: Elemental Magic for St. Patrick's Day

Clover Chronicles: Finding Your Inner Luck

Ireland's Mystical Creatures: A Field Guide

Gingerbread Golem's Love Almanac

Prowl and Thrive: The Lion's Guide to Success

Love Alchemy: Transforming Your Life Through Heart Energy

WORLD DOMINATION: Woman's Rule 3:The New Life

The Midnight Rose: A Guide to Lunar Love Spells

The Forbidden Letters: Writing Your Own Love Prophecy

Luck and Lore: St. Patrick's Day for Modern Mystics

The Green Path: A Pagan Celebration of Renewal

The Dark Architect's Guide to Reprogramming Reality

Prankster's Paradise: A Guide to Harmless Hijinks

Manifest Your Reality: The Law of Attraction Simplified

The TARDIS Owner's Manual: Understanding the Doctor's Ship: *A complete guide to the TARDIS, its technology, secrets, and mysteries*

Starlit Romance: Astrology Secrets for Finding True Love

The Time Lord's Atlas: A Complete Guide to the Whoniverse: *A breakdown of the locations, planets, and dimensions explored in Doctor Who*

Sweetheart Shadows: The Dark Side of Love and Attraction

February Fire: Reigniting Passion in Every Area of Life

The Self-Love Toolkit: 5 Ways to Embrace Who You Are

February Sparks: Ignite Your Dreams in 28 Days

March to Success: A 31-Day Action Blueprint

Ancient Paths: The 13 Sacred Principles of Dino Wicca

Echoes of Tomorrow: Navigating the AI Revolution

The Wellness Blueprint: Balancing Mind, Body, and Soul

Green Horizons: Sustainable Living for a Better Tomorrow

The AI Wealth Code: How to Make Millions with Automation

AI-Powered Creativity: Writing, Art, and Music for Profit

Extinction Rites: Rebirthing Your Soul Through Prehistoric Magick

Sacred Serpents tarot

Celestial Enchantment blank journal

Star Strains

Culinary Journeys: Exploring Global Flavors at Home

The Hollowvale Curse

The Hollowvale Harvest

The Egg of Transformation: Awakening Your Inner Power

Blooming Into Power: A Wiccan Guide to Spring Awakening

The Nightmare Nexus: The Third Doctor's Perilous Haunting

Digital Detox: Reclaiming Your Life in a Connected World

Ostara's Path: Walking the Spiral of Renewal

The Sacred Hare

Financial Freedom: Building Wealth in the Modern Age

Spring's Cauldron: Stirring the Waters of Change

The Hollowvale Pact

Quantum Consciousness: The Science of Reality Shifting

The Hollowvale Hunger

The Sacred Waters Within: A Witch's Guide to Hydrocephalus Magick

The Raven's Nest: Building a Life of Unshakable Stability

AI and the Human Mind: The Future of Intelligence

The Hollowvale Reckoning

Timeless Love: Building and Maintaining Lasting Relationships

The Raven's Roar: Unlocking Unstoppable Confidence

Raven Sight: Awakening Intuition and Inner Wisdom

The Butterfly Effect: Small Changes, Big Transformations

Taming the Boogeyman: How to Conquer Your Inner Fears

The Magick of Green: Awakening Earth's Energy in You

The Entrepreneurial Mindset: Secrets to Business Success

The Hollowvale End

The Shadow Luck Ritual: Reclaiming Power from Your Dark Side

Spring Magick for Beginners: A Simple Guide to Seasonal Energy Work

Doctor Who: The Hollowvale Conundrum

The March of Miracles: Unlocking Synchronicities in Spring

Unveiling the Cosmos: A Guide to Stargazing and Space Exploration

The Ultimate Guide to Surviving an Economic Collapse

The AI Gold Rush: How to Profit from the AI Revolution

Bastet's Shadow: The Hidden Power of Feline Magick

The Bastet Codex: Unlocking the Goddess's Magickal Secrets

Purring Spells: Harnessing Bastet's Healing Frequencies

Bastet's Nine Lives: Rebirth, Transformation, and Immortality Spells

Primal Currents: Hydrocephalus Magick in the Path of Dino Wicca

The Digital Gold Rush: Mastering E-Commerce and Online Sales

Future Shock: Adapting to the Next Decade of Change

The Quantum Mindset: Think Like a Billionaire

Sacred Motherhood: Awakening the Divine Feminine Within

The Mother's Spellbook: Enchantments for Love, Protection, and Prosperity

The Witch's Guide to Parenting: Raising Empowered and Intuitive Children

The Magick of Motherhood: Reclaiming Your Power Through Rituals

The Pagan Path to Self-Love: A Goddess's Guide to Worth and Confidence

Wild Woman Magick: Unleashing Your Primal Power

The Money Magnet Blueprint: Unlocking Unlimited Wealth

Biohacking 101: Unlock Your Body's Full Potential

The Wild Father: A Pagan Guide to Strength and Wisdom

The Sacred Masculine: Unlocking Your Inner Power

The Druid's Compass

The Warrior's Mindset

The Father's Fire

Odin's Path

Ancestral Bonds

The House That Whispers

The Magician's Code

The Wild Hunt

The Green Man's Path

The Altar of Success

The Shadow and the Sword

The High Priestess's Guide to Energy Healing

The Lunar Mother

The Sacred Self-Care Grimoire

The Womb Wisdom Codex

The Wheel of the Mother

The Witch's Guide to Manifestation

The Q2 Reset

The Ultimate Guide to AI-Powered Passive Income

Escape the 9-5

AI Feline Fortunes

The Tear-Stained Grimoire

Razorblade Runes

Cemetery Sirens

The Midnight Wristwatch
The Town That Forgets
AI Horror & Creepypasta
The Hollow Frequency
The Breach Echo
The Quiet Between Worlds
The Sigil of Tharan-Khul
Summon the Vault of Y'ha'ten
The Becoming Codex
The Profit of Az'ra-nar
The Drowned Logos
Echoes of the Eldritch Will
The Deep Ledger
Necronomicon of Networth
Covenant of the Wealthwyrm
The Whisperer's Manifesto
The Rites of Azh-K'luth
The Ark of the Crawling Coin
The Tithe of Shadows
Inkheart Abyss
The Timewinds of Y'ha-nthlei
The Spiral Labyrinth of Azag-Nirrh
The Gallifreyan Heresy of the Black Pharaoh
The Psalms of Nyog-Sotha
Black Rain Alchemy
The Infinite Maw
The Entropic Blueprint
The Oracle of Sh'guul
The Book of Breach
The Drowned Saint's Testament
Dreamcraft of the Sleeper God
The Silence Market
Cthonomics: The Dark Wealth Algorithm

Invocation of the Ten-Eyed King
Wealthbound to the Wyrm Below
Become the Unnameable
Codex of the Sovereign Flame
Rituals of Relentless Becoming
The Shadow Ascends
The Eyes Beneath You
The Will That Wakes Worlds
Silence Is a Weapon
The Mirror That Screams
The Whisper Between Moments
The Mind That Devours Fear
The Myth of the Finished Self
The Architect of Your Madness
The Voice You've Buried
The Discipline of Madness
Stormborn: Awakening Your Inner Tempest
The Mind That Ate Time
Unbind Your Becoming
The Pact You Owe Yourself
The Devourer's Diet
The Acid That Carves the Path
The Tower You Must Burn
The Breath Between Worlds
Speak Like the Deep
The Labyrinth Within
The Spine of the Sea God
Rejection Is a Portal
The Crown You Refused
The Scar Is the Spell
The Lightless Flame
The Habit of Becoming Horrific
ChickenJockey Chaos

The Gatekeeper Within

You Are Not Your Name

The Compass of the Mad

The Archive of Unsent Letters

What the Mirror Can't Show You

The Knife You Needed

Worship Nothing, Become Everything

The Other Voice

The Body the World Forgot

The Vein of the Void

The Black Bone Codex

The Puzzle of the Hidden Self (Millennium Puzzle)

The Eye That Sees the Lie *(Millennium Eye)*

The Ring of Return (Millennium Ring)

The Rod of Relentless Will *(Millennium Rod)*

The Tally of the Soul (Millennium Tauk/Necklace)

The Key to the Locked Timeline (Millennium Key)

The Scale of Sacred Decisions (Millennium Scales)

Inferno Bites: The UnOfficial Minecraft Lava Cookbook

Rot in the Attic

Prana: The Hidden Force of Your Infinite Self

The Shadow Realm Within: Transforming Darkness Into Destiny

The Borderland Collapse

Claws of Protection: Bastet's Defensive Magick

Mr. Ring-a-Ding's Madness

Yugioh Astrology: Celestial Deckcraft and Duel Destiny (2026–2027 Edition)

The Seal You Signed: Unlocking the Power You Once Feared

The Puzzle of Infinite Minds: Unlocking the Mentalism Hidden Within

The Eye That Mirrors the All: Secrets of Inner Reflection

Doctor Who: The Toymaker's Broadcast

Rootwake: The Carbon Covenant

Skitter Logic: Unlearning the Fear That Built You

Doctor Who: The World That Froths

Rootwake: The Fizz That Rewrites Flesh

Rootwake: Frothfather of the World

The Holly Pact: Blood Beneath the Mistletoe

The 2nd Mass Principle: Building Unbreakable Tribes

Web of Wits: A Survival Guide to Encounters with Anasi the Spider (Aunt Nancy)

The Hexbreaking Handbook: Effective Spells to Remove Curses

Pop Alchemy: Transform Your Life One Sip at a Time

The Mason Code: Leading in Unleadable Times

Petosiris and the Fifth Chamber of Thoth

The Ether Seed Within

The Parent of Tomorrow

Petosiris's Pyramid of Perpetual Wealth

Unlearn the World

Grimoire of the Hollow Tongue

Zodiac Weeds: Finding Your Strain Through the Stars

Aquarius Rises in the Bank

The Sugar God's Smile

The Skinclock Reversal: Biohacking the Face of Time

Debtburn: How to Obliterate What You Owe Forever

The Ice Cream Oracle: What Your Cone Says About Your Future

Silence Is Sovereignty: The Power of Being Unreadable

The Wind That Whispers Through Stone

Path of the Four Directions

Doctor Who: The Maestro's Symphony of Endings

Oxygen Grail: Breathing to Undo the Clock

Zodiacal Collapse: When Stars Devour Time

Teachings from the Red Sand Silence

Doctor Who: Omega – The Broken Equation
Memory Wipe Your Past: Start Over Like a MiB
Mitochondria Prime: Ignite the Core of Youth
A Nest of Roaches
Grub from the Galaxy: MiB Recipes You'll Never Forget

Get Some Tarot cards: https://www.makeplayingcards.com/sell/apophis-occult-shop

Get some shirts: https://www.bonfire.com/store/apophis-shirt-emporium/

<u>Instagrams:</u>
@apophis_enterprises,
@apophisbookemporium,
@apophisscardshop
Twitter: @apophisenterpr1
Tiktok:@apophisenterprise
Youtube: @sg1fan23477
Hive: @sg1fan23477
CheeLee: @SG1fan23477

Podcast: Apophis Chat Zone: https://open.spotify.com/show/5zXbrCLEV2xzCp8ybrfHsk?si=fb4d4fdbdce44dec

Newsletter: https://apophiss-newsletter-27c897.beehiiv.com/

If you want to support me or see posts of other projects that I have come over to: **buymeacoffee.com/mpetchinskg**
I post there daily several times a day

Get your Dinowicca or Christmas themed digital products, especially Santa Raptor songs and other musics. Here: **https://sg1fan23477.gumroad.com**

Apophis Yuletide Digital has not only digital Christmas items, but it will have all things with Dinowicca as well as other Digital products.